CELEBRATING HOLIDAYS

Passover

by Rachel Grack

BLASTOFF!
READERS
2

BELLWETHER MEDIA • MINNEAPOLIS, MN

Note to Librarians, Teachers, and Parents:

Blastoff! Readers are carefully developed by literacy experts and combine standards-based content with developmentally appropriate text.

Level 1 provides the most support through repetition of high-frequency words, light text, predictable sentence patterns, and strong visual support.

Level 2 offers early readers a bit more challenge through varied simple sentences, increased text load, and less repetition of high-frequency words.

Level 3 advances early-fluent readers toward fluency through increased text and concept load, less reliance on visuals, longer sentences, and more literary language.

Level 4 builds reading stamina by providing more text per page, increased use of punctuation, greater variation in sentence patterns, and increasingly challenging vocabulary.

Level 5 encourages children to move from "learning to read" to "reading to learn" by providing even more text, varied writing styles, and less familiar topics.

Whichever book is right for your reader, Blastoff! Readers are the perfect books to build confidence and encourage a love of reading that will last a lifetime!

This edition first published in 2019 by Bellwether Media, Inc.

No part of this publication may be reproduced in whole or in part without written permission of the publisher. For information regarding permission, write to Bellwether Media, Inc., Attention: Permissions Department, 6012 Blue Circle Drive, Minnetonka, MN 55343.

Library of Congress Cataloging-in-Publication Data

Names: Koestler-Grack, Rachel A., 1973- author.
Title: Passover / by Rachel Grack.
Description: Minneapolis, MN : Bellwether Media, Inc., [2019] | Series: Blastoff! Readers: Celebrating Holidays | Includes bibliographical references and index. | Audience: Ages 5-8. | Audience: K-3.
Identifiers: LCCN 2017056568 (print) | LCCN 2017057044 (ebook) | ISBN 9781626177901 (hardcover : alk. paper) | ISBN 9781681035192 (ebook)
Subjects: LCSH: Passover–Juvenile literature.
Classification: LCC BM695.P3 (ebook) | LCC BM695.P3 K575 2019 (print) | DDC 296.4/37–dc23
LC record available at https://lccn.loc.gov/2017056568

Editor: Paige Polinsky   Designer: Andrea Schneider

Printed in the United States of America, North Mankato, MN.

Table of Contents

Children run from room to room. They are on a **matzah** hunt!

matzah

The child who finds this hidden bread gets a prize. It is Passover!

What Is Passover?

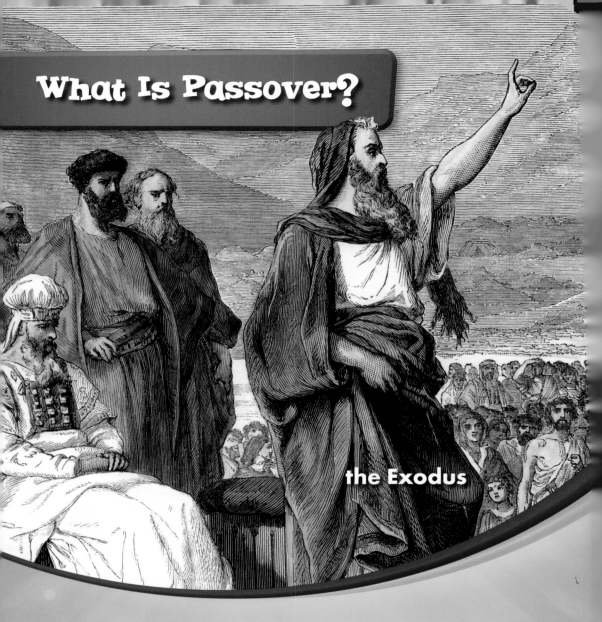

the Exodus

Passover is a **Jewish** holiday. It celebrates the **Exodus** of the Jewish people.

It also marks the
start of spring.

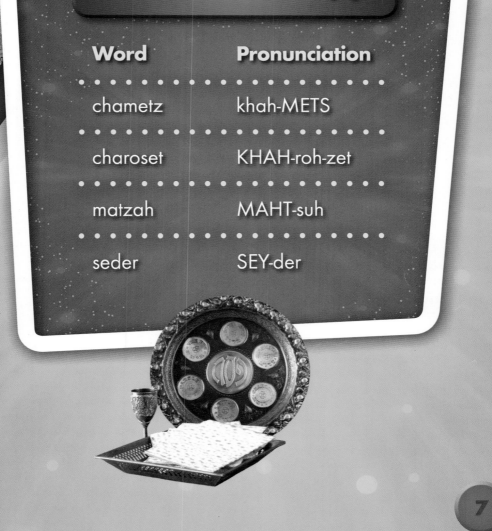

How Do You Say?

Word	Pronunciation
chametz	khah-METS
charoset	KHAH-roh-zet
matzah	MAHT-suh
seder	SEY-der

Who Celebrates Passover?

Jews honor this holiday. They remember how God freed their **ancestors**.

Jerusalem, Israel

Jews in Israel celebrate for seven days. In other countries, Passover lasts eight days.

Passover Beginnings

Egypt

Passover began more than 3,000 years ago. The Jews were **slaves** in Egypt.

God promised to free them.
He sent ten **plagues** to
punish the Egyptians.

modern Egypt

All firstborn sons died in the last plague. But the Jews marked their doors with lambs' blood.

Jewish family marks door

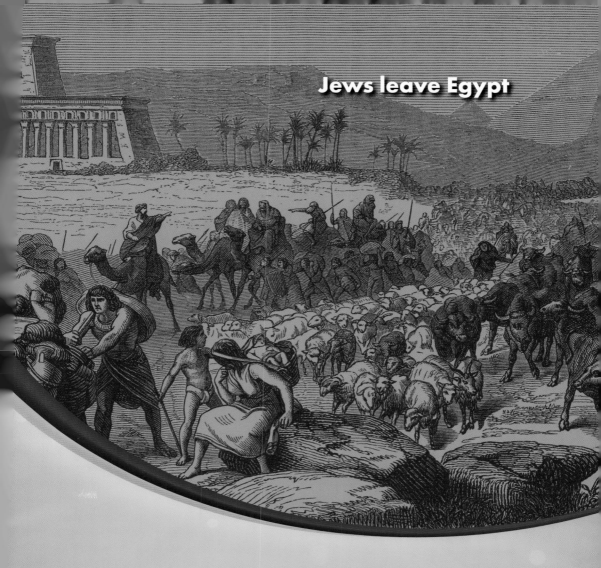

Jews leave Egypt

God passed over their
homes. Their sons were safe.
The **Pharaoh** let them go!

Passover is in April or May. It follows the **Hebrew** calendar.

The holiday starts on day 15 of the month Nissan.

Passover Traditions!

Families clean their homes. They get rid of all **chametz**.

family burns
chametz

They light a special candle to welcome Passover.

Passover starts with the *seder*. This meal follows a set order. Each food has a special meaning. Families tell the Exodus story while they eat.

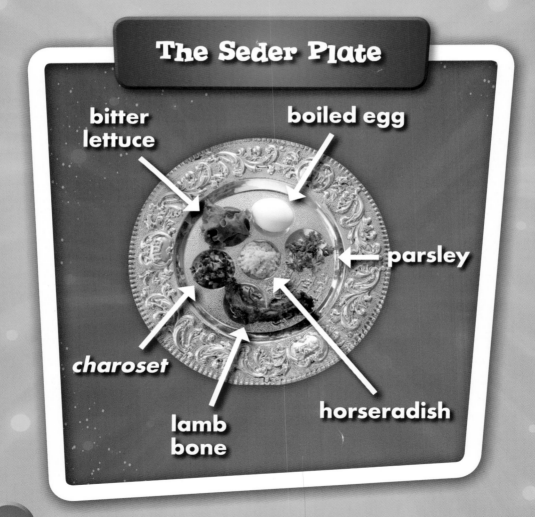

The Seder Plate

bitter lettuce

boiled egg

parsley

charoset

lamb bone

horseradish

Make Charoset!

Charoset is served at the Passover seder. It stands for the clay Jews used to build bricks when they were slaves.

Recipe

What You Need:
- red apple
- pear
- ½ cup raisins
- 1 cup chopped walnuts
- ¼ teaspoon cinnamon
- ½ cup grape juice
- bowl
- vegetable peeler
- knife
- cutting board
- measuring cups
- measuring spoons
- mixing spoon

What You Do:
1. Have an adult help you peel the apple and pear.
2. Have an adult help you finely chop the fruit.
3. Add all ingredients to the bowl.
4. Stir to mix. Then serve!

People say prayers and sing **hymns**. Children talk about why Passover is special.

Jews celebrate their freedom!

Glossary

ancestors—relatives who lived long ago

chametz—anything made with wheat, rye, barley, oats, or spelt that has been allowed to rise for more than 18 minutes

Exodus—the events that took place when the Jews left Egypt

Hebrew—Jewish; Jews are also called Hebrews.

hymns—songs of worship and praise

Jewish—related to Judaism, a religion that began in Israel and teaches belief in one God

matzah—a crisp, flat bread made without yeast

Pharaoh—the ruler of Egypt

plagues—horrible happenings that affect a great number of people; the ten plagues of Egypt included illness, fire, and insects.

punish—to make someone suffer for a crime or for bad behavior

slaves—people who are considered property

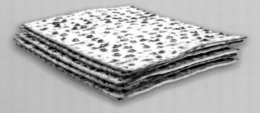

To Learn More

AT THE LIBRARY

Adler, David A. *The Story of Passover*. New York, N.Y.: Holiday House, 2014.

Gillespie, Katie. *Passover*. New York, N.Y.: AV2 by Weigl, 2015.

Grack, Rachel. *Hanukkah*. Minneapolis, Minn.: Bellwether Media, 2017.

ON THE WEB

Learning more about Passover is as easy as 1, 2, 3.

1. Go to www.factsurfer.com.

2. Enter "Passover" into the search box.

3. Click the "Surf" button and you will see a list of related web sites.

With factsurfer.com, finding more information is just a click away.

Index

The images in this book are reproduced through the courtesy of: DanGonzalez, front cover, p. 18; PeopleImages, p. 4; Africa Studio, pp. 4-5; Noam Armonn, pp. 4-5, 20-21; North Wind Picture Archives/ Alamy, pp. 6-7, 12; tomertu, p. 7, 22; Gosiek-B, p. 8; Sean Pavone, pp. 8-9; Orhan Cam, pp. 10-11; ZU_09, pp. 12-13; JodiJacobson, pp. 14-15; Golden Pixels LLC, p. 15; RnDmS, p. 16; ZUMA Press, Inc./ Alamy, pp. 16-17; Andrea Schneider/ Bellwether Media, p. 19; kali9, p. 20.